151213

SPORTS THROUGHOUT HISTORY™

The History of
HOCKEY

Diana Star Helmer and Thomas S. Owens

The Rosen Publishing Group's
PowerKids Press™
New York

Published in 2000 by The Rosen Publishing Group, Inc.
29 East 21st Street, New York, NY 10010

Copyright © 2000 by The Rosen Publishing Group, Inc.

First Edition

Book Design: Michael de Guzman

Photo Credits: pp. 4, 7, 8 CORBIS-Bettmann; p. 11 © Allsport, Reuters/CORBIS-Bettmann, and CORBIS/ Sean Sexton Collection; p. 12 © Reuters/Jason Cohn/Archive Photos; p. 15 © Al Bello/Allsport, © Vincent Laforet/Allsport, © AP Wide World Photos, and Reuters/CORBIS-Bettmann; pp. 16, 20 © AP Wide World Photos; p. 18 CORBIS/Paul A. Souders.

Helmer, Diana Star, 1962-
     The history of hockey / by Diana Star Helmer and Thomas S. Owens.
          p.   cm.
     Includes index.
     Summary: Discusses the history of ice hockey in Canada and the United States from the 1800s to today, including its popularity, leagues, and notable players.
     ISBN 0-8239-5468-4 (lib. bdg.: alk. paper)
     1. Hockey—Canada—History—Juvenile literature. 2. Hockey—United States—History—Juvenile literature. [1. Hockey—History.] I. Owens, Tom, 1960- . II. Title. III. Series: Helmer, Diana Star, 1962-
Sports throughout history.
GV847.25.H45 1999
796.962'097—dc21   99-12136
                                                                      CIP
                                                                        AC

Manufactured in the United States of America

Contents

*Starting in the 1700s, people in Scotland played an early
hockey game that was similar to hurling, called shinny.*

Early Hockey Games

   People around the world are very different, but their games are often alike. As early as 1200 B.C., people in Ireland played a game called **hurling**. Players hit a leather ball along the ground and through the air with a stick called a hurley. In Canada in the early 1800s, the Mimac Indians played a game like hurling, but it was on ice and used a square wooden block instead of a ball. These games were some of the early forms of hockey.

5

Playing on Ice

In the 1600s, the English sent explorers, soldiers, and settlers to Canada to claim land for England. By the 1850s, many English, Irish, and Scottish people had moved to Canada. People still played their old games, like hurling. In Canada, where the winters are long and snowy, they had to play them on ice. This is how ice hockey began. The first known official hockey game was played in 1855 by British soldiers on the frozen layers of ice on Lake Ontario.

Today most people play hockey on ice rinks instead of on frozen lakes. Playing on a lake can be dangerous since it is possible for someone to fall through the ice and into the cold water. ▶

It's Official

British soldiers traveled across Canada. As they crossed the country, they taught hockey to others. Since there was no one to make official rules, people in different towns played different ways. In 1875, students from Canada's McGill University wrote down rules for hockey. Hockey spread quickly. Just ten years later, in 1885, teams from all over Canada set up hockey's first national **league**. It was called the **Amateur** Hockey Association.

◀ *Players in amateur hockey leagues play for fun, not money.*

The Stanley Cup

As hockey spread, it gained more and more fans. Canada's **governor general**, Lord Stanley, and his sons loved to watch the game. In 1893, Lord Stanley bought a **trophy** to give to Canada's best hockey club. Every year, teams could try for the prize.

Today, the Stanley Cup is hockey's greatest award. The first Stanley Cup cost $48.33. Back then, that was a lot of money. It wasn't the cost of the prize that was important, though. To players then and now, winning the Cup is priceless.

A picture of Lord Stanley is shown here next to the Stanley Cup. ▶

The Professionals

Hockey began in the 1800s as an amateur sport. At that time, people didn't think it was right to play for money. Fans loved games enough to buy tickets, though, and great players wanted to spend more time at practice than at other jobs. Slowly, fans came to accept **professional** sports. The International Pro Hockey League was started in 1904, with U.S. and Canadian teams. This league didn't last long, but it was hockey's first professional group.

◄ *Today, teams like the Pittsburgh Penguins and the St. Louis Blues are made up of professional hockey players.*

Bigger and Better

The National Hockey League started in 1917 with four Canadian teams. In 1924, the first American team, the Boston Bruins, entered the league. Then more U.S. teams joined. In 1967, the NHL grew from six teams to twelve. In 1972, a new league, the World

▶ Mike Keane, of the *Dallas Stars.*

Wayne Gretzky, of the New York Rangers.

Hockey Association, formed with twelve teams of its own. The two leagues fought over the best players. When the WHA ended the 1978-79 season with money problems, the two leagues combined. The NHL adopted four WHA teams. Today the NHL has 21 teams.

Sergei Krivourasov, of the Nashville Predators.

Mario Lemieux, of the Pittsburgh Penguins.

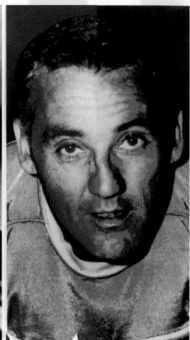
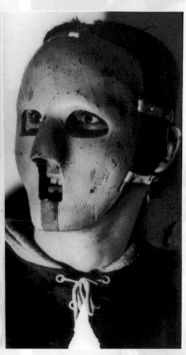

Jacques Plante

Happy Accidents

Hockey has changed a lot over time, sometimes by accident. In 1904, team size was set at six after a team came to a game without the usual nine players. In 1959, **goalie** Jacques Plante said he wouldn't play without a mask after a puck hit him in the face. Other goalies began wearing masks for safety, too. In 1960, Stan Mikita bent the blade of his stick but kept practicing. The curved stick sent the puck flying! Soon, everyone wanted "banana blades."

◀ *Jacques Plante made hockey safer for all players by insisting that he be allowed to wear a mask.*

Kids' Play

In Canada, hockey leagues for kids are very popular. In 1955, Ab Hoffman was the best player on a Canadian boys' team. When coaches found out Ab was a girl, she really became a star! Today, both boys and girls in Canada can play in hockey leagues, beginning at age five. More than 650,000 kids play on youth teams there. The United States has youth hockey leagues, too. While most players live in the coldest parts of America, teams exist in all 50 states.

◀ *Even warm states like Florida and Hawaii have ice hockey for kids.*

Check out Women in Hockey

Women played hockey almost from the start. In the 1900s, women played on college teams. Back then, women wore skirts during games and were not allowed to play rough. Women's hockey still does not allow **body checking**. Many fans believe women's hockey is more exciting because of the no checking rule. **Shooting** and **passing** matter most. Some women even play on men's teams. In the 1990s, Manon Rhéaume and Erin Whitten became goalies on men's professional teams.

◀ *Manon Rhéaume plays for the Tampa Bay Lightning.*

Best in the World

Although hockey began in Canada, it is now a popular sport all over the world. Today there are teams in countries like Finland, Thailand, and Ecuador.

The Detroit Red Wings, who won the Stanley Cup in 1998, had players from five different countries. Hockey is a sport that brings people together.

Web Sites:

Check out this Web site on hockey:
http://www.wintersports.org/hockey/index.html

Glossary

amateur (A-muh-chur) Someone who does something as a hobby but not as a job.

body checking (BAH-dee CHEH-king) Hitting a player with your body to stop him from moving forward or scoring.

goalie (GOH-lee) The person who guards the goal to keep the other team from scoring.

governor general (GUH-vuh-nur JEN-rul) A political leader of a state or large territory.

hurling (HUR-ling) An Irish game that was like field hockey.

league (LEEG) A group of teams that play against each other in the same sport.

passing (PA-sing) Hitting the puck to a teammate.

professional (pruh-FEH-shuh-nul) When an activity is done as a job, not just for fun.

shooting (SHOO-ting) Trying to hit the puck into the goal to score a point.

trophy (TROH-fee) An award that is often made of metal and shaped like a cup.

Index